MW01088497

CAMPING
and
TRAMPING
with
ROOSEVELT

THE PRESIDENT ON GLACIER POINT, YOSEMITE VALLEY

CAMPING
and
TRAMPING
with
ROOSEVELT

John Burroughs

Dover Publications, Inc.
Mineola, New York

Bibliographical Note

This Dover edition, first published in 2017, is an unabridged republication of the work originally published in 1907 by Houghton, Mifflin and Company, Boston and New York.

This book contains twelve photographs, all of which were originally stereographs. Five of the photographs have been moved to a new position within the text.

Library of Congress Cataloging-in-Publication Data

Names: Burroughs, John, 1837–1921, author.
Title: Camping and tramping with Roosevelt / John Burroughs.
Other titles: Camping & tramping with Roosevelt
Description: Mineola, New York : Dover Publications, Inc., 2017. | "An unabridged republication of the work originally published in 1907 by Houghton, Mifflin and Company, Boston and New York"—Title page verso.
Identifiers: LCCN 2016051407| ISBN 9780486812540 (paperback) | ISBN 0486812545 (paperback)
Subjects: LCSH: Roosevelt, Theodore, 1858-1919—Travel—Yellowstone National Park. | Burroughs, John, 1837–1921--Travel—Yellowstone National Park. | Yellowstone National Park—Description and travel. | Natural history—Yellowstone National Park. | Presidents—United States—Biography. | Naturalists—United States—Biography. | Roosevelt, Theodore, 1858-1919—Philosophy. | Philosophy of nature—United States. | BISAC: BIOGRAPHY & AUTOBIOGRAPHY / Personal Memoirs. | HISTORY / Essays. |
HISTORY / United States / State & Local / Pacific Northwest (OR, WA).
Classification: LCC E757 .B97 2017 | DDC 973.91/1092—dc23 LC record available at https://lccn.loc.gov/2016051407

Manufactured in the United States by LSC Communications
81254501   2017
www.doverpublications.com

ILLUSTRATIONS

INTRODUCTION

THIS little volume really needs no introduction; the two sketches of which it is made explain and, I hope, justify themselves. But there is one phase of the President's many-sided character upon which I should like to lay especial emphasis, namely, his natural history bent and knowledge. Amid all his absorbing interests and masterful activities in other fields, his interest and his authority in practical natural history are by no means the least. I long ago had very direct proof of this statement. In some of my English sketches, following a visit to that island in 1882, I had, rather by implication than by positive statement, inclined to the opinion that the European forms of animal life were, as a rule, larger and more hardy and prolific than the corresponding forms in this country. Roosevelt could not let this statement or suggestion go unchallenged, and the letter which I received from him in 1892, touching these things, is of double interest at this time, as showing one phase of his radical Americanism, while it exhibits him as a thoroughgoing naturalist. I am sure my readers will welcome the gist of this letter. After some preliminary remarks he says: —

"The point of which I am speaking is where you say that the Old World forms of animal life are coarser, stronger, fiercer, and more fertile than those of the New World." (My statement was not quite so sweeping as this.) "Now I don't think that this is so; at least, comparing the forms which are typical of North America and of northern Asia and Europe, which together form but one province of animal life.

INTRODUCTION

"Many animals and birds which increase very fast in new countries, and which are commonly spoken of as European in their origin, are really as alien to Europe as to their new homes. Thus the rabbit, rat, and mouse are just as truly interlopers in England as in the United States and Australia, having moved thither apparently within historic times, the rabbit from North Africa, the others from southern Asia; and one could no more generalize upon the comparative weakness of the American fauna from these cases of intruders than one could generalize from them upon the comparative weakness of the British, German, and French wild animals. Our wood mouse or deer mouse retreats before the ordinary house mouse in exactly the same way that the European wood mouse does, and not a whit more. Our big wood rat stands in the same relation to the house rat. Casting aside these cases, it seems to me, looking at the mammals, that it would be quite impossible to generalize as to whether those of the Old or the New World are more fecund, are the fiercest, the hardiest, or the strongest. A great many cases could be cited on both sides. Our moose and caribou are, in certain of their varieties, rather larger than the Old World forms of the same species. If there is any difference between the beavers of the two countries, it is in the same direction. So with the great family of the field mice. The largest true arvicola seems to be the yellow-cheeked mouse of Hudson's Bay, and the biggest representative of the family on either continent is the muskrat. In most of its varieties the wolf of North America seems to be inferior in strength and courage to that of northern Europe and Asia; but the direct reverse is true with the grizzly bear, which

is merely a somewhat larger and fiercer
variety of the common European brown
bear. On the whole, the Old World bison,
or so-called aurochs, appears to be somewhat more formidable than its American
brother; but the difference against the
latter is not anything like as great as the
difference in favor of the American wapiti,
which is nothing but a giant representative of the comparatively puny European stag. So with the red fox. The fox
of New York is about the size of that
of France, and inferior in size to that of
Scotland; the latter in turn is inferior in
size to the big fox of the upper Missouri,
while the largest of all comes from British
America. There is no basis for the belief
that the red fox was imported here from
Europe; its skin was a common article
of trade with the Canadian fur traders
from the earliest times. On the other
hand, the European lynx is much bigger

than the American. The weasels afford cases in point, showing how hard it is to make a general law on the subject. The American badger is very much smaller than the European, and the American otter very much larger than the European otter. Our pine marten, or sable, compared with that of Europe, shows the very qualities of which you speak; that is, its skull is slenderer, the bones are somewhat lighter, the teeth less stout, the form showing more grace and less strength. But curiously enough this is reversed, with even greater emphasis, in the minks of the two continents, the American being much the largest and strongest, with stouter teeth, bigger bones, and a stronger animal in every way. The little weasel is on the whole smaller here, while the big weasel, or stoat, is, in some of its varieties at least, largest on this side; and, of the true weasels, the largest of all is the so-called fisher, a purely American beast, a fierce and hardy animal which habitually preys upon as hard fighting a creature as the raccoon, and which could eat all the Asiatic and European varieties of weasels without an effort.

"About birds I should be far less competent to advance arguments, and especially, my dear sir, to you; but it seems to me that two of the most self-asserting and hardiest of our families of birds are the tyrant flycatchers, of which the kingbird is chief, and the blackbirds, or grackles, with the meadow lark at their head, both characteristically American.

"Did you ever look over the medical statistics of the half million men drafted during the Civil War? They include men of every race and color, and from every country of Europe, and from every State in the Union; and so many men were measured that the average of the measurements is probably pretty fair. From these it would appear that the physical type in the Eastern States had undoubtedly degenerated. The man from New York or New England, unless he came from the lumbering districts, though as tall as the Englishman or Irishman, was distinctly lighter built, and especially was narrower across the chest; but the finest men physically of all were the Kentuckians and Tennesseeans. After them came the Scandinavians, then the Scotch, then the people from several of the Western States, such as Wisconsin and Minnesota, then the Irish, then the Germans, then the English, etc. The decay of vitality, especially as shown in the decreasing fertility of the New England and, indeed, New York stock, is very alarming; but the most prolific peoples on this continent, whether of native or foreign origin, are the native whites of the southern

Alleghany region in Kentucky and Tennessee, the Virginians, and the Carolinians, and also the French of Canada.

"It will be difficult to frame a general law of fecundity in comparing the effects upon human life of long residence on the two continents when we see that the Frenchman in Canada is healthy and enormously fertile, while the old French stock is at the stationary point in France, the direct reverse being the case when the English of Old and of New England are compared, and the decision being again reversed if we compare the English with the mountain whites of the Southern States."

CAMPING WITH
PRESIDENT ROOSEVELT

CAMPING WITH
PRESIDENT ROOSEVELT

At the time I made the trip to Yellowstone Park with President Roosevelt in the spring of 1903, I promised some friends to write up my impressions of the President and of the Park, but I have been slow in getting around to it. The President himself, having the absolute leisure and peace of the White House, wrote his account of the trip nearly two years ago! But with the stress and strain of my life at "Slabsides," — administering the affairs of so many of the wild creatures of the woods about me, — I have not till this blessed season (fall of 1905) found the time to put on record an account of the most interesting thing I saw in that wonderful land, which, of course, was the President himself.

When I accepted his invitation I was well aware that during the journey I should be in a storm centre most of the time, which is not always a pleasant prospect to a man of my habits and disposition. The President himself is a good deal of a storm, — a man of such abounding energy and ceaseless activity that he sets everything in motion around him wherever he goes. But I knew he would be pretty well occupied on his way to the Park in speaking to eager throngs and in receiving personal and political homage in the towns and cities we were to pass through. But when all this was over, and I found myself with him in the wilderness of the Park, with only the superintendent and a few attendants to help take up his tremendous personal impact, how was it likely to fare with a non-strenuous person like myself? I asked. I had visions of snow six and seven feet deep, where

4

traveling could be done only upon snow-shoes, and I had never had the things on my feet in my life. If the infernal fires beneath, that keep the pot boiling so furiously in the Park, should melt the snows, I could see the party tearing along on horseback at a wolf-hunt pace over a rough country; and as I had not been on a horse's back since the President was born, how would it be likely to fare with me then?

I had known the President several years before he became famous, and we had had some correspondence on subjects of natural history. His interest in such themes is always very fresh and keen, and the main motive of his visit to the Park at this time was to see and study in its semi-domesticated condition the great game which he had so often hunted during his ranch days; and he was kind enough to think it would be an additional

5

pleasure to see it with a nature-lover like myself. For my own part, I knew nothing about big game, but I knew there was no man in the country with whom I should so like to see it as Roosevelt.

Some of our newspapers reported that the President intended to hunt in the Park. A woman in Vermont wrote me, to protest against the hunting, and hoped I would teach the President to love the animals as much as I did, — as if he did not love them much more, because his love is founded upon knowledge, and because they had been a part of his life. She did not know that I was then cherishing the secret hope that I might be allowed to shoot a cougar or bobcat; but this fun did not come to me. The President said, "I will not fire a gun in the Park; then I shall have no explanations to make." Yet once I did hear him say in the wilderness, "I feel as if I ought to

6

keep the camp in meat. I always have."
I regretted that he could not do so on this
occasion.

I have never been disturbed by the
President's hunting trips. It is to such
men as he that the big game legitimately
belongs, — men who regard it from the
point of view of the naturalist as well as
from that of the sportsman, who are in-
terested in its preservation, and who share
with the world the delight they experience
in the chase. Such a hunter as Roosevelt
is as far removed from the game-butcher
as day is from night; and as for his killing of the "varmints," — bears, cougars,
and bobcats, — the fewer of these there
are, the better for the useful and beautiful
game.

The cougars, or mountain lions, in the
Park certainly needed killing. The superintendent reported that he had seen where
they had slain nineteen elk, and we saw

where they had killed a deer and dragged its body across the trail. Of course, the President would not now on his hunting trips shoot an elk or a deer except to "keep the camp in meat," and for this purpose it is as legitimate as to slay a sheep or a steer for the table at home.

We left Washington on April 1, and strung several of the larger Western cities on our thread of travel, — Chicago, Milwaukee, Madison, St. Paul, Minneapolis, — as well as many lesser towns, in each of which the President made an address, sometimes brief, on a few occasions of an hour or more.

He gave himself very freely and heartily to the people wherever he went. He could easily match their Western cordiality and good-fellowship. Wherever his train stopped, crowds soon gathered, or had already gathered, to welcome him. His advent made a holiday in each town he visited. At all the principal stops the usual programme was: first, his reception by the committee of citizens appointed to receive him, — they usually boarded his private car, and were one by one introduced to him; then a drive through the town with a concourse of carriages; then to the hall or open-air platform, where he spoke to the assembled throng; then to lunch or dinner; and then back to the train, and off for the next stop, — a round of hand-shaking, carriage-driving, speech-making each day. He usually spoke from eight to ten times every twenty-four hours, sometimes for only a few minutes from the rear platform of his private car, at others for an hour or more in some large hall. In Chicago, Milwaukee, and St. Paul, elaborate banquets were given him and his party, and on each occasion he delivered a carefully prepared speech upon questions that involved the policy of his administration. The throng that greeted him in the vast Auditorium in Chicago — that rose and waved and waved again — was one of the grandest human spectacles I ever witnessed.

In Milwaukee the dense cloud of tobacco smoke that presently filled the large hall after the feasting was over was enough to choke any speaker, but it did not seem to choke the President, though he does not use tobacco in any form himself; nor was there anything foggy about his utterances on that occasion upon legislative control of the trusts.

In St. Paul the city was inundated with humanity, — a vast human tide that left the middle of the streets bare as our line of carriages moved slowly along, but that rose up in solid walls of town and prairie humanity on the sidewalks and city dooryards. How hearty and happy the myriad faces looked! At one

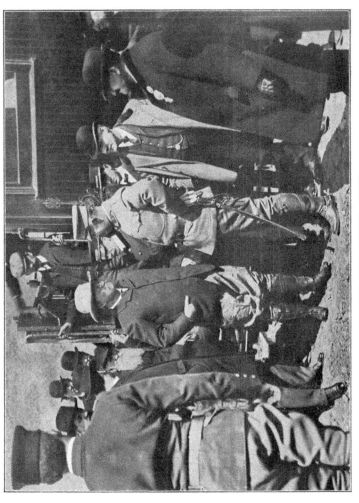

ARRIVAL AT GARDINER, MONT.
(ENTRANCE TO YELLOWSTONE NATIONAL PARK.)

THE PRESIDENT WITH MR. BURROUGHS AND SECRETARY LOEB
JUST BEFORE ENTERING THE PARK.

point I spied in the throng on the curb-stone a large silk banner that bore my own name as the title of some society. I presently saw that it was borne by half a dozen anxious and expectant-looking schoolgirls with braids down their backs. As my carriage drew near them, they pressed their way through the throng and threw a large bouquet of flowers into my lap. I think it would be hard to say who blushed the deeper, the girls or myself. It was the first time I had ever had flowers showered upon me in public; and then, maybe, I felt that on such an occasion I was only a minor side issue, and public recognition was not called for. But the incident pleased the President. "I saw that banner and those flowers," he said afterwards; "and I was delighted to see you honored that way." But I fear I have not to this day thanked the Monroe School of St. Paul for that pretty attention.

The time of the passing of the presidential train seemed well known, even on the Dakota prairies. At one point I remember a little brown schoolhouse stood not far off, and near the track the school-ma'am, with her flock, drawn up in line. We were at luncheon, but the President caught a glimpse ahead through the window, and quickly took in the situation. With napkin in hand, he rushed out on the platform and waved to them. "Those children," he said, as he came back, "wanted to see the President of the United States, and I could not disappoint them. They may never have another chance. What a deep impression such things make when we are young!"

At some point in the Dakotas we picked up the former foreman of his ranch and another cowboy friend of the old days, and they rode with the President in his private car for several hours. He was as happy with them as a schoolboy ever was in meeting old chums. He beamed with delight all over. The life which those men represented, and of which he had himself once formed a part, meant so much to him; it had entered into the very marrow of his being, and I could see the joy of it all shining in his face as he sat and lived parts of it over again with those men that day. He bubbled with laughter continually. The men, I thought, seemed a little embarrassed by his open-handed cordiality and good-fellowship. He himself evidently wanted to forget the present, and to live only in the memory of those wonderful ranch days, — that free, hardy, adventurous life upon the plains. It all came back to him with a rush when he found himself alone with these heroes of the rope and the stirrup. How much more keen his appreciation was, and how much quicker his memory, than theirs!

13

He was constantly recalling to their minds incidents which they had forgotten, and the names of horses and dogs which had escaped them. His subsequent life, instead of making dim the memory of his ranch days, seemed to have made it more vivid by contrast.

When they had gone I said to him, "I think your affection for those men very beautiful."

"How could I help it?" he said.

"Still, few men in your station could or would go back and renew such friendships."

"Then I pity them," he replied.

He said afterwards that his ranch life had been the making of him. It had built him up and hardened him physically, and it had opened his eyes to the wealth of manly character among the plainsmen and cattlemen.

Had he not gone West, he said, he

never would have raised the Rough Riders
regiment; and had he not raised that
regiment and gone to the Cuban War, he
would not have been made governor of
New York; and had not this happened,
the politicians would not unwittingly
have made his rise to the Presidency so
inevitable. There is no doubt, I think,
that he would have got there some day;
but without the chain of events above
outlined, his rise could not have been so
rapid.

Our train entered the Bad Lands of
North Dakota in the early evening twi-
light, and the President stood on the rear
platform of his car, gazing wistfully upon
the scene. "I know all this country like a
book," he said. "I have ridden over it,
and hunted over it, and tramped over it,
in all seasons and weather, and it looks
like home to me. My old ranch is not
far off. We shall soon reach Medora,

which was my station." It was plain to see that that strange, forbidding-looking landscape, hills and valleys to eastern eyes, utterly demoralized and gone to the bad, — flayed, fantastic, treeless, a riot of naked clay slopes, chimney-like buttes, and dry coulees, — was in his eyes a land of almost pathetic interest. There were streaks of good pasturage here and there where his cattle used to graze, and where the deer and the pronghorn used to linger.

When we reached Medora, where the train was scheduled to stop an hour, it was nearly dark, but the whole town and country round had turned out to welcome their old townsman. After much hand-shaking, the committee conducted us down to a little hall, where the President stood on a low platform, and made a short address to the standing crowd that filled the place. Then some flashlight pictures were taken by the local photographer, after which the President stepped down, and, while the people filed past him, shook hands with every man, woman, and child of them, calling many of them by name, and greeting them all most cordially. I recall one grizzled old frontiersman whose hand he grasped, calling him by name, and saying, "How well I remember you! You once mended my gunlock for me, — put on a new hammer." "Yes," said the delighted old fellow; "I'm the man, Mr. President." He was among his old neighbors once more, and the pleasure of the meeting was very obvious on both sides. I heard one of the women tell him they were going to have a dance presently, and ask him if he would not stay and open it! The President laughingly excused himself, and said his train had to leave on schedule time, and his time was nearly up. I thought of the incident in his "Ranch Life," in which he says he once opened a cowboy ball with the wife of a Minnesota man, who danced opposite, and who had recently shot a bullying Scotchman. He says the scene reminded him of the ball where Bret Harte's heroine "went down the middle with the man that shot Sandy Magee."

Before reaching Medora he had told me many anecdotes of "Hell-Roaring Bill Jones," and had said I should see him. But it turned out that Hell-Roaring Bill had begun to celebrate the coming of the President too early in the day, and when we reached Medora he was not in a presentable condition. I forget now how he had earned his name, but no doubt he had come honestly by it; it was a part of his history, as was that of "The Pike," "Cold-Turkey Bill," "Hash-Knife Joe," and other classic heroes of the frontier.

It is curious how certain things go to the bad in the Far West, or a certain proportion of them, — bad lands, bad horses, and bad men. And it is a degree of badness that the East has no conception of, — land that looks as raw and unnatural as if time had never laid its shaping and softening hand upon it; horses that, when mounted, put their heads to the ground and their heels in the air, and, squealing defiantly, resort to the most diabolically ingenious tricks to shake off or to kill their riders; and men who amuse themselves in bar-rooms by shooting about the feet of a "tenderfoot." to make him dance, or who ride along the street and shoot at every one in sight. Just as the old plutonic fires come to the surface out there in the Rockies, and hint very strongly of the infernal regions, so a kind of satanic element in men and animals — an underlying devilishness — crops out, and we have the border ruffian and the bucking broncho.

The President told of an Englishman on a hunting trip in the West, who, being an expert horseman at home, scorned the idea that he could not ride any of their "grass-fed ponies." So they gave him a bucking broncho. He was soon lying on the ground, much stunned. When he could speak, he said, "I should not have minded him, you know, *but 'e 'ides 'is 'ead.*"

At one place in Dakota the train stopped to take water while we were at lunch. A crowd soon gathered, and the President went out to greet them. We could hear his voice, and the cheers and laughter of the crowd. And then we heard him say, "Well, good-by, I must go now." Still he did not come. Then we heard more talking and laughing, and another "good-by," and yet he did not come. Then I

went out to see what had happened. I
found the President down on the ground
shaking hands with the whole lot of them.
Some one had reached up to shake his
hand as he was about withdrawing, and
this had been followed by such eagerness
on the part of the rest of the people to do
likewise, that the President had instantly
got down to gratify them. Had the secret
service men known it, they would have
been in a pickle. We probably have never
had a President who responded more
freely and heartily to the popular liking
for him than Roosevelt. The crowd always seem to be in love with him the
moment they see him and hear his voice.
And it is not by reason of any arts of elo-
quence, or charm of address, but by reason of his inborn heartiness and sincerity,
and his genuine manliness. The people
feel his quality at once. In Bermuda last
winter I met a Catholic priest who had

sat on the platform at some place in New England very near the President while he was speaking, and who said, "The man had not spoken three minutes before I loved him, and had any one tried to molest him, I could have torn him to pieces." It is the quality in the man that instantly inspires such a liking as this in strangers that will, I am sure, safeguard him in all public places.

I once heard him say that he did not like to be addressed as "His Excellency;" he added laughingly, "They might just as well call me 'His Transparency,' for all I care." It is this transparency, this direct out-and-out, unequivocal character of him that is one source of his popularity. The people do love transparency, — all of them but the politicians.

A friend of his one day took him to task for some mistake he had made in one of his appointments. "My dear sir," replied the President, "where you know of one mistake I have made, I know of ten." How such candor must make the politicians shiver!

I have said that I stood in dread of the necessity of snowshoeing in the Park, and, in lieu of that, of horseback riding. Yet when we reached Gardiner, the entrance to the Park, on that bright, crisp April morning, with no snow in sight save that on the mountain-tops, and found Major Pitcher and Captain Chittenden at the head of a squad of soldiers, with a fine saddle-horse for the President, and an ambulance drawn by two span of mules for me, I confess that I experienced just a slight shade of mortification. I thought they might have given me the option of the saddle or the ambulance. Yet I entered the vehicle as if it was just what I had been expecting.

The President and his escort, with a

cloud of cowboys hovering in the rear, were soon off at a lively pace, and my ambulance followed close, and at a lively pace, too; so lively that I soon found myself gripping the seat with both hands. "Well," I said to myself, "they are giving me a regular Western send-off;" and I thought, as the ambulance swayed from side to side, that it would suit me just as well if my driver did not try to keep up with the presidential procession. The driver and his mules were shut off from me by a curtain, but, looking ahead out of the sides of the vehicle, I saw two good-sized logs lying across our course. Surely, I thought (and barely had time to think), he will avoid these. But he did not, and as we passed over them I was nearly thrown through the top of the ambulance. "This *is* a lively send-off," I said, rubbing my bruises with one hand, while I clung to the seat with the other. Presently I

24

saw the cowboys scrambling up the bank as if to get out of our way; then the President on his fine gray stallion scrambling up the bank with his escort, and looking ominously in my direction, as we thundered by.

"Well," I said, "this is indeed a novel ride; for once in my life I have sidetracked the President of the United States! I am given the right of way over all." On we tore, along the smooth, hard road, and did not slacken our pace till, at the end of a mile or two, we began to mount the hill toward Fort Yellowstone. And not till we reached the fort did I learn that our mules had run away. They had been excited beyond control by the presidential cavalcade, and the driver, finding he could not hold them, had aimed only to keep them in the road, and we very soon had the road all to ourselves.

Fort Yellowstone is at Mammoth Hot Springs, where one gets his first view of the characteristic scenery of the Park, — huge, boiling springs with their columns of vapor, and the first characteristic odors which suggest the traditional infernal regions quite as much as the boiling and steaming water does. One also gets a taste of a much more rarefied air than he has been used to, and finds himself panting for breath on a very slight exertion. The Mammoth Hot Springs have built themselves up an enormous mound that stands there above the village on the side of the mountain, terraced and scalloped and fluted, and suggesting some vitreous formation, or rare carving of enormous, many-colored precious stones. It looks quite unearthly, and, though the devil's frying pan, and ink pot, and the Stygian caves are not far off, the suggestion is of something celestial rather than of the nether regions, — a vision of jasper walls, and of amethyst battlements.

With Captain Chittenden I climbed to the top, stepping over the rills and creeks of steaming hot water, and looked at the marvelously clear, cerulean, but boiling, pools on the summit. The water seemed as unearthly in its beauty and purity as the gigantic sculpturing that held it.

The Stygian caves are still farther up the mountain, — little pockets in the rocks, or well-holes in the ground at your feet, filled with deadly carbon dioxide. We saw birds' feathers and quills in all of them. The birds hop into them, probably in quest of food or seeking shelter, and they never come out. We saw the body of a martin on the bank of one hole. Into one we sank a lighted torch, and it was extinguished as quickly as if we had dropped it into water. Each cave or niche is a death valley on a small scale. Near by

27

we came upon a steaming pool, or lakelet, of an acre or more in extent. A pair of mallard ducks were swimming about in one end of it, — the cool end. When we approached, they swam slowly over into the warmer water. As they progressed, the water got hotter and hotter, and the ducks' discomfort was evident. Presently they stopped, and turned towards us, half appealingly, as I thought. They could go no farther; would we please come no nearer? As I took another step or two, up they rose and disappeared over the hill. Had they gone to the extreme end of the pool, we could have had boiled mallard for dinner.

Another novel spectacle was at night, or near sundown, when the deer came down from the hills into the streets and ate hay, a few yards from the officers' quarters, as unconcernedly as so many domestic sheep. This they had been doing all winter, and they kept it up till May, at times a score or more of them profiting thus on the government's bounty. When the sundown gun was fired a couple of hundred yards away, they gave a nervous start, but kept on with their feeding. The antelope and elk and mountain sheep had not yet grown bold enough to accept Uncle Sam's charity in that way.

The President wanted all the freedom and solitude possible while in the Park, so all newspaper men and other strangers were excluded. Even the secret service men and his physician and private secretaries were left at Gardiner. He craved once more to be alone with nature; he was evidently hungry for the wild and the aboriginal, — a hunger that seems to come upon him regularly at least once a year, and drives him forth on his hunting trips for big game in the West.

We spent two weeks in the Park, and had fair weather, bright, crisp days, and clear, freezing nights. The first week we occupied three camps that had been prepared, or partly prepared, for us in the northeast corner of the Park, in the region drained by the Gardiner River, where there was but little snow, and which we reached on horseback.

The second week we visited the geyser region, which lies a thousand feet or more higher, and where the snow was still five or six feet deep. This part of the journey was made in big sleighs, each drawn by two span of horses.

On the horseback excursion, which involved only about fifty miles of riding, we had a mule pack train, and Sibley tents and stoves, with quite a retinue of camp laborers, a lieutenant and an orderly or two, and a guide, Billy Hofer.

The first camp was in a wild, rocky,

and picturesque gorge on the Yellow-stone, about ten miles from the fort. A slight indisposition, the result of luxurious living, with no wood to chop or to saw, and no hills to climb, as at home, pre-vented me from joining the party till the third day. Then Captain Chittenden drove me eight miles in a buggy. About two miles from camp we came to a picket of two or three soldiers, where my big bay was in waiting for me. I mounted him confidently, and, guided by an or-derly, took the narrow, winding trail toward camp. Except for an hour's riding the day before with Captain Chittenden, I had not been on a horse's back for nearly fifty years, and I had not spent as much as a day in the saddle during my youth. That first sense of a live, spirited, powerful animal beneath you, at whose mercy you are, — you, a pedestrian all your days, — with gullies and rocks and logs to cross, and deep chasms opening close beside you, is not a little disturbing. But my big bay did his part well, and I did not lose my head or my nerve, as we cautiously made our way along the narrow path on the side of the steep gorge, with a foaming torrent rushing along at its foot, nor yet when we forded the rocky and rapid Yellowstone. A misstep or a stumble on the part of my steed, and probably the first bubble of my confidence would have been shivered at once; but this did not happen, and in due time we reached the group of tents that formed the President's camp.

The situation was delightful, — no snow, scattered pine trees, a secluded valley, rocky heights, and the clear, ample, trouty waters of the Yellowstone. The President was not in camp. In the morning he had stated his wish to go alone into the wilderness. Major Pitcher very naturally did not quite like the idea, and wished to send an orderly with him.

"No," said the President. "Put me up a lunch, and let me go alone. I will surely come back."

And back he surely came. It was about five o'clock when he came briskly down the path from the east to the camp. It came out that he had tramped about eighteen miles through a very rough country. The day before, he and the major had located a band of several hundred elk on a broad, treeless hillside, and his purpose was to find those elk, and creep up on them, and eat his lunch under their very noses. And this he did, spending an hour or more within fifty yards of them. He came back looking as fresh as when he started, and at night, sitting before the big camp fire, related his adventure, and talked with his usual emphasis and copiousness of many things.

33

He told me of the birds he had seen or heard; among them he had heard one that was new to him. From his description I told him I thought it was Townsend's solitaire, a bird I much wanted to see and hear. I had heard the West India solitaire, — one of the most impressive songsters I ever heard, — and I wished to compare our Western form with it.

The next morning we set out for our second camp, ten or a dozen miles away, and in reaching it passed over much of the ground the President had traversed the day before. As we came to a wild, rocky place above a deep chasm of the river, with a few scattered pine trees, the President said, "It was right here that I heard that strange bird song." We paused a moment. "And there it is now!" he exclaimed.

Sure enough, there was the solitaire singing from the top of a small cedar, —

34

a bright, animated, eloquent song, but without the richness and magic of the song of the tropical species. We hitched our horses, and followed the bird up as it flew from tree to tree. The President was as eager to see and hear it as I was. It seemed very shy, and we only caught glimpses of it. In form and color it much resembles its West India cousin, and suggests our catbird. It ceased to sing when we pursued it. It is a bird found only in the wilder and higher parts of the Rockies. My impression was that its song did not quite merit the encomiums that have been pronounced upon it.

At this point, I saw amid the rocks my first and only Rocky Mountain wood-chucks, and, soon after we had resumed our journey, our first blue grouse, — a number of them like larger partridges. Occasionally we would come upon black-tailed deer, standing or lying down in the

35

bushes, their large ears at attention being the first thing to catch the eye. They would often allow us to pass within a few rods of them without showing alarm. Elk horns were scattered all over this part of the Park, and we passed several old carcasses of dead elk that had probably died a natural death.

In a grassy bottom at the foot of a steep hill, while the President and I were dismounted, and noting the pleasing picture which our pack train of fifteen or twenty mules made filing along the side of a steep grassy slope, — a picture which he has preserved in his late volume, "Out-Door Pastimes of an American Hunter," — our attention was attracted by plaintive, musical, bird-like chirps that rose from the grass about us. I was almost certain it was made by a bird; the President was of like opinion; and we kicked about in the tufts of grass, hoping to flush

36

the bird. Now here, now there, arose this sharp, but bird-like note. Finally, we found that it was made by a species of gopher, whose holes we soon discovered. What its specific name is I do not know, but it should be called the singing gopher.

Our destination this day was a camp on Cottonwood Creek, near "Hell-Roaring Creek." As we made our way in the afternoon along a broad, open, grassy valley, I saw a horseman come galloping over the hill to our right, starting up a band of elk as he came; riding across the plain, he wheeled his horse, and, with the military salute, joined our party. He proved to be a government scout, called the "Duke of Hell Roaring," — an educated officer from the Austrian army, who, for some unknown reason, had exiled himself here in this out-of-the-way part of the world. He was a man in his prime, of fine, military look and bearing. After conversing a few moments with the President and Major Pitcher, he rode rapidly away.

Our second camp, which we reached in mid-afternoon, was in the edge of the woods on the banks of a fine, large trout stream, where ice and snow still lingered in patches. I tried for trout in the head of a large, partly open pool, but did not get a rise; too much ice in the stream, I concluded. Very soon my attention was attracted by a strange note, or call, in the spruce woods. The President had also noticed it, and, with me, wondered what made it. Was it bird or beast? Billy Hofer said he thought it was an owl, but the sound in no way suggested an owl, and the sun was shining brightly. It was a sound such as a boy might make by blowing in the neck of an empty bottle. Presently we heard it beyond us on the

THE PRESIDENT IN THE BEAR COUNTRY

MR. BURROUGHS'S FAVORITE PASTIME.

other side of the creek, which was pretty good proof that the creature had wings.

"Let's go run that bird down," said the President to me.

So off we started across a small, open, snow-streaked plain, toward the woods beyond it. We soon decided that the bird was on the top of one of a group of tall spruces. After much skipping about over logs and rocks, and much craning of our necks, we made him out on the peak of a spruce. I imitated his call, when he turned his head down toward us, but we could not make out what he was.

"Why did we not think to bring the glasses?" said the President.

"I will run and get them," I replied.

"No," said he, "you stay here and keep that bird treed, and I will fetch them."

So off he went like a boy, and was very soon back with the glasses. We quickly made out that it was indeed an owl, —

39

the pigmy owl, as it turned out, — not much larger than a bluebird. I think the President was as pleased as if we had bagged some big game. He had never seen the bird before.

Throughout the trip I found his interest in bird life very keen, and his eye and ear remarkably quick. He usually saw the bird or heard its note as quickly as I did, — and I had nothing else to think about, and had been teaching my eye and ear the trick of it for over fifty years. Of course, his training as a big-game hunter stood him in good stead, but back of that were his naturalist's instincts, and his genuine love of all forms of wild life.

I have been told that his ambition up to the time he went to Harvard had been to be a naturalist, but that there they seem to have convinced him that all the out-of-door worlds of natural history had been conquered, and that the only worlds remaining were in the laboratory, and to be won with the microscope and the scalpel. But Roosevelt was a man made for action in a wide field, and laboratory conquests could not satisfy him. His instincts as a naturalist, however, lie back of all his hunting expeditions, and, in a large measure, I think, prompt them. Certain it is that his hunting records contain more live natural history than any similar records known to me, unless it be those of Charles St. John, the Scotch naturalist-sportsman.

The Canada jays, or camp-robbers, as they are often called, soon found out our camp that afternoon, and no sooner had the cook begun to throw out peelings and scraps and crusts than the jays began to carry them off, not to eat, as I observed, but to hide them in the thicker branches of the spruce trees. How tame they were, coming within three or four yards of one! Why this species of jay should everywhere be so familiar, and all other kinds so wild, is a puzzle.

In the morning, as we rode down the valley toward our next camping-place, at Tower Falls, a band of elk containing a hundred or more started along the side of the hill a few hundred yards away. I was some distance behind the rest of the party, as usual, when I saw the President wheel his horse off to the left, and, beckoning to me to follow, start at a tearing pace on the trail of the fleeing elk. He afterwards told me that he wanted me to get a good view of those elk at close range, and he was afraid that if he sent the major or Hofer to lead me, I would not get it. I hurried along as fast as I could, which was not fast; the way was rough, — logs, rocks, spring runs, and a tenderfoot rider.

Now and then the President, looking back and seeing what slow progress I was making, would beckon to me impatiently, and I could fancy him saying, "If I had a rope around him, he would come faster than that!" Once or twice I lost sight of both him and the elk; the altitude was great, and the horse was laboring like a steam engine on an upgrade. Still I urged him on. Presently, as I broke over a hill, I saw the President pressing the elk up the opposite slope. At the brow of the hill he stopped, and I soon joined him. There on the top, not fifty yards away, stood the elk in a mass, their heads toward us and their tongues hanging out. They could run no farther. The President laughed like a boy. The spectacle meant much more to him than it did to me. I had never seen a wild elk till on this trip, but they had been among the notable game that he had hunted. He had traveled hundreds of miles, and undergone great hardships, to get within rifle range of these creatures. Now here stood scores

43

of them with lolling tongues, begging for mercy.

After gazing at them to our hearts' content, we turned away to look up our companions, who were nowhere within sight. We finally spied them a mile or more away, and, joining them, all made our way to an elevated plateau that commanded an open landscape three or four miles across. It was high noon, and the sun shone clear and warm. From this lookout we saw herds upon herds of elk scattered over the slopes and gentle valleys in front of us. Some were grazing, some were standing or lying upon the ground, or upon the patches of snow. Through our glasses we counted the separate bands, and then the numbers of some of the bands or groups, and estimated that three thousand elk were in full view in the landscape around us. It was a notable spectacle. Afterward, in Montana, I attended a council of Indian chiefs at one of the Indian agencies, and told them, through their interpreter, that I had been with the Great Chief in the Park, and of the game we had seen. When I told them of these three thousand elk all in view at once, they grunted loudly, whether with satisfaction or with incredulity, I could not tell.

In the midst of this great game amphitheatre we dismounted and enjoyed the prospect. And the President did an unusual thing, he loafed for nearly an hour, — stretched himself out in the sunshine upon a flat rock, as did the rest of us, and, I hope, got a few winks of sleep. I am sure I did. Little, slender, striped chipmunks, about half the size of ours, were scurrying about; but I recall no other wild things save the elk.

From here we rode down the valley to our third camp, at Tower Falls, stopping on the way to eat our luncheon on a washed boulder beside a creek. On this ride I saw my first and only badger; he stuck his striped head out of his hole in the ground only a few yards away from us as we passed.

Our camp at Tower Falls was amid the spruces above a cañon of the Yellowstone, five or six hundred feet deep. It was a beautiful and impressive situation, — shelter, snugness, even cosiness, — looking over the brink of the awful and the terrifying. With a run and a jump I think one might have landed in the river at the bottom of the great abyss, and in doing so might have scaled one of those natural obelisks or needles of rock that stand up out of the depths two or three hundred feet high. Nature shows you what an enormous furrow her plough can open through the strata when moving horizontally, at the same time that she shows you what delicate and graceful columns her slower and gentler aerial forces can carve out of the piled strata. At the Falls there were two or three of these columns, like the picket-pins of the elder gods.

Across the cañon in front of our camp, upon a grassy plateau which was faced by a wall of trap rock, apparently thirty or forty feet high, a band of mountain sheep soon attracted our attention. They were within long rifle range, but were not at all disturbed by our presence, nor had they been disturbed by the road-builders who, under Captain Chittenden, were constructing a government road along the brink of the cañon. We speculated as to whether or not the sheep could get down the almost perpendicular face of the chasm to the river to drink. It seemed to me impossible. Would they try it while we were there to see? We all hoped so; and sure enough, late in the afternoon

47

the word came to our tents that the sheep were coming down. The President, with coat off and a towel around his neck, was shaving. One side of his face was half shaved, and the other side lathered. Hofer and I started for a point on the brink of the cañon where we could have a better view.

"By Jove," said the President, "I must see that. The shaving can wait, and the sheep won't."

So on he came, accoutred as he was, — coatless, hatless, but not latherless, nor towelless. Like the rest of us, his only thought was to see those sheep do their "stunt." With glasses in hand, we watched them descend those perilous heights, leaping from point to point, finding a foothold where none appeared to our eyes, loosening fragments of the crumbling rocks as they came, now poised upon some narrow shelf and preparing for the next leap, zig-zagging or plunging straight down till the bottom was reached, and not one accident or misstep amid all that insecure footing. I think the President was the most pleased of us all; he laughed with the delight of it, and quite forgot his need of a hat and coat till I sent for them.

In the night we heard the sheep going back; we could tell by the noise of the falling stones. In the morning I confidently expected to see some of them lying dead at the foot of the cliffs, but there they all were at the top once more, apparently safe and sound. They do, however, occasionally meet with accidents in their perilous climbing, and their dead bodies have been found at the foot of the rocks. Doubtless some point of rock to which they had trusted gave way, and crushed them in the descent, or fell upon those in the lead.

The next day, while the rest of us went fishing for trout in the Yellowstone, three or four miles above the camp, over the roughest trail that we had yet traversed on horseback, the President, who never fishes unless put to it for meat, went off alone again with his lunch in his pocket, to stalk those sheep as he had stalked the elk, and to feel the old sportsman's thrill without the use of firearms. To do this involved a tramp of eight or ten miles down the river to a bridge and up the opposite bank. This he did, and ate his lunch near the sheep, and was back in camp before we were.

We took some large cut-throat trout, as they are called, from the yellow mark across their throats, and I saw at short range a black-tailed deer bounding along in that curious, stiff-legged, mechanical, yet springy manner, apparently all four legs in the air at once, and all four feet reaching the ground at once, affording a very singular spectacle.

We spent two nights in our Tower Falls camp, and on the morning of the third day set out on our return to Fort Yellowstone, pausing at Yancey's on our way, and exchanging greetings with the old frontiersman, who died a few weeks later.

While in camp we always had a big fire at night in the open near the tents, and around this we sat upon logs or campstools, and listened to the President's talk. What a stream of it he poured forth! and what a varied and picturesque stream! — anecdote, history, science, politics, adventure, literature; bits of his experience as a ranchman, hunter, Rough Rider, legislator, civil service commissioner, police commissioner, governor, president, —the frankest confessions, the most telling criticisms, happy characterizations of prominent political leaders, or foreign rulers, or members of his own Cabinet; always surprising by his candor, aston-

ishing by his memory, and diverting by
his humor. His reading has been very
wide, and he has that rare type of memory which retains details as well as mass
and generalities. One night something
started him off on ancient history, and
one would have thought he was just fresh
from his college course in history, the dates
and names and events came so readily.
Another time he discussed palæontology,
and rapidly gave the outlines of the science,
and the main facts, as if he had been reading up on the subject that very day. He
sees things as wholes, and hence the relation of the parts comes easy to him.

At dinner, at the White House, the
night before we started on the expedition,
I heard him talking with a guest, — an
officer of the British army, who was just
back from India. And the extent and variety of his information about India and
Indian history and the relations of the

British government to it were extraordinary. It put the British major on his mettle to keep pace with him.

One night in camp he told us the story of one of his Rough Riders who had just written him from some place in Arizona. The Rough Riders, wherever they are now, look to him in time of trouble. This one had come to grief in Arizona. He was in jail. So he wrote the President, and his letter ran something like this: —

"DEAR COLONEL, — I am in trouble. I shot a lady in the eye, but I did not intend to hit the lady; I was shooting at my wife."

And the presidential laughter rang out over the tree-tops. To another Rough Rider, who was in jail, accused of horse stealing, he had loaned two hundred dollars to pay counsel on his trial, and, to his surprise, in due time the money

53

came back. The ex-Rough wrote that his trial never came off. "*We elected our district attorney;*" and the laughter again sounded, and drowned the noise of the brook near by.

On another occasion we asked the President if he was ever molested by any of the "bad men" of the frontier, with whom he had often come in contact. "Only once," he said. The cowboys had always treated him with the utmost courtesy, both on the round-up and in camp; "and the few real desperadoes I have seen were also perfectly polite." Once only was he maliciously shot at, and then not by a cowboy nor a *bona fide* "bad man," but by a "broad-hatted ruffian of a cheap and common-place type." He had been compelled to pass the night at a little frontier hotel where the bar-room occupied the whole lower floor, and was, in consequence, the only place where the guests of the

54

hotel, whether drunk or sober, could sit. As he entered the room, he saw that every man there was being terrorized by a half-drunken ruffian who stood in the middle of the floor with a revolver in each hand, compelling different ones to treat.

"I went and sat down behind the stove," said the President, "as far from him as I could get; and hoped to escape his notice. The fact that I wore glasses, together with my evident desire to avoid a fight, apparently gave him the impression that I could be imposed upon with impunity. He very soon approached me, flourishing his two guns, and ordered me to treat. I made no reply for some moments, when the fellow became so threatening that I saw something had to be done. The crowd, mostly sheep-herders and small grangers, sat or stood back against the wall, afraid to move. I was unarmed, and thought rapidly. Saying, 'Well, if I

55

must, I must,' I got up as if to walk around him to the bar, then, as I got opposite him, I wheeled and fetched him as heavy a blow on the chin-point as I could strike. He went down like a steer before the axe, firing both guns into the ceiling as he went. I jumped on him, and, with my knees on his chest, disarmed him in a hurry. The crowd was then ready enough to help me, and we hog-tied him and put him in an outhouse." The President alludes to this incident in his "Ranch Life," but does not give the details. It brings out his mettle very distinctly.

He told us in an amused way of the attempts of his political opponents at Albany, during his early career as a member of the Assembly, to besmirch his character. His outspoken criticisms and denunciations had become intolerable to them, so they laid a trap for him, but he was not caught. His innate rectitude and instinct for the right course saved him, as it has saved him many times since. I do not think that in any emergency he has to debate with himself long as to the right course to be pursued; he divines it by a kind of infallible instinct. His motives are so simple and direct that he finds a straight and easy course where another man, whose eye is less single, would flounder and hesitate.

One night he entertained us with reminiscences of the Cuban War, of his efforts to get his men to the firing line when the fighting began, of his greenness and general ignorance of the whole business of war, which in his telling was very amusing. He has probably put it all in his book about the war, a work I have not yet read. He described the look of the slope of Kettle Hill when they were about to charge up it, how the grass was combed and rippled by the storm of rifle bullets that swept down it. He said, "I was conscious of being pale when I looked at it and knew that in a few moments we were going to charge there." The men of his regiment were all lying flat upon the ground, and it became his duty to walk along their front and encourage them and order them up on their feet. "Get up, men, get up!" One big fellow did not rise. Roosevelt stooped down and took hold of him and ordered him up. Just at that moment a bullet struck the man and went the entire length of him. He never rose.

On this or on another occasion when a charge was ordered, he found himself a hundred yards or more in advance of his regiment, with only the color bearer and one corporal with him. He said they planted the flag there, while he rushed back to fetch the men. He was evidently pretty hot. "Can it be that you flinched when I led the way!" and then they came with a rush. On the summit of Kettle Hill he was again in advance of his men, and as he came up, three Spaniards rose out of the trenches and deliberately fired at him at a distance of only a few paces, and then turned and fled. But a bullet from his revolver stopped one of them. He seems to have been as much exposed to bullets in this engagement as Washington was at Braddock's defeat, and to have escaped in the same marvelous manner.

The President unites in himself powers and qualities that rarely go together. Thus, he has both physical and moral courage in a degree rare in history. He can stand calm and unflinching in the path of a charging grizzly, and he can confront with equal coolness and determination the predaceous corporations and money powers of the country.

He unites the qualities of the man of action with those of the scholar and writer,

59

— another very rare combination. He unites the instincts and accomplishments of the best breeding and culture with the broadest democratic sympathies and affiliations. He is as happy with a frontiersman like Seth Bullock as with a fellow Harvard man, and Seth Bullock is happy, too.

He unites great austerity with great good nature. He unites great sensibility with great force and will power. He loves solitude, and he loves to be in the thick of the fight. His love of nature is equaled only by his love of the ways and marts of men.

He is doubtless the most vital man on the continent, if not on the planet, to-day. He is many-sided, and every side throbs with his tremendous life and energy; the pressure is equal all around. His interests are as keen in natural history as in economics, in literature as in statecraft, in the young poet as in the old soldier, in preserving peace as in preparing for war. And he can turn all his great power into the new channel on the instant. His interest in the whole of life, and in the whole life of the nation, never flags for a moment. His activity is tireless. All the relaxation he needs or craves is a change of work. He is like the farmer's fields, that only need a rotation of crops. I once heard him say that all he cared about being President was just "the big work."

During this tour through the West, lasting over two months, he made nearly three hundred speeches; and yet on his return Mrs. Roosevelt told me he looked as fresh and unworn as when he left home.

We went up into the big geyser region with the big sleighs, each drawn by four horses. A big snow-bank had to be shoveled through for us before we got to the

61

Golden Gate, two miles above Mammoth Hot Springs. Beyond that we were at an altitude of about eight thousand feet, on a fairly level course that led now through woods, and now through open country, with the snow of a uniform depth of four or five feet, except as we neared the "formations," where the subterranean warmth kept the ground bare. The roads had been broken and the snow packed for us by teams from the fort, otherwise the journey would have been impossible.

The President always rode beside the driver. From his youth, he said, this seat had always been the most desirable one to him. When the sleigh would strike the bare ground, and begin to drag heavily, he would bound out nimbly and take to his heels, and then all three of us — Major Pitcher, Mr. Childs, and myself — would follow suit, sometimes reluctantly on my part. Walking at that altitude is no fun, especially if you try to keep pace with such a walker as the President is. But he could not sit at his ease and let those horses drag him in a sleigh over bare ground. When snow was reached, we would again quickly resume our seats.

As one nears the geyser region, he gets the impression from the columns of steam going up here and there in the distance — now from behind a piece of woods, now from out a hidden valley — that he is approaching a manufacturing centre, or a railroad terminus. And when he begins to hear the hoarse snoring of "Roaring Mountain," the illusion is still more complete. At Norris's there is a big vent where the steam comes tearing out of a recent hole in the ground with terrific force. Huge mounds of ice had formed from the congealed vapor all around it, some of them very striking.

The novelty of the geyser region soon

wears off. Steam and hot water are steam and hot water the world over, and the exhibition of them here did not differ, except in volume, from what one sees by his own fireside. The "Growler" is only a boiling tea-kettle on a large scale, and "Old Faithful" is as if the lid were to fly off, and the whole contents of the kettle should be thrown high into the air. To be sure, boiling lakes and steaming rivers are not common, but the new features seemed, somehow, out of place, and as if nature had made a mistake. One disliked to see so much good steam and hot water going to waste; whole towns might be warmed by them, and big wheels made to go round. I wondered that they had not piped them into the big hotels which they opened for us, and which were warmed by wood fires.

At Norris's the big room that the President and I occupied was on the ground

SUNRISE IN YELLOWSTONE PARK.

THE PRESIDENT ON A TRAIL

floor, and was heated by a huge box stove. As we entered it to go to bed, the President said, "Oom John, don't you think it is too hot here?"

"I certainly do," I replied.

"Shall I open the window?"

"That will just suit me." And he threw the sash, which came down to the floor, all the way up, making an opening like a doorway. The night was cold, but neither of us suffered from the abundance of fresh air.

The caretaker of the building was a big Swede called Andy. In the morning Andy said that beat him: "There was the President of the United States sleeping in that room, with the window open to the floor, and not so much as one soldier outside on guard."

The President had counted much on seeing the bears that in summer board at the Fountain Hotel, but they were not yet out of their dens. We saw the track of only one, and he was not making for the hotel. At all the formations where the geysers are, the ground was bare over a large area. I even saw a wild flower — an early buttercup, not an inch high — in bloom. This seems to be the earliest wild flower in the Rockies. It is the only fragrant buttercup I know.

As we were riding along in our big sleigh toward the Fountain Hotel, the President suddenly jumped out, and, with his soft hat as a shield to his hand, captured a mouse that was running along over the ground near us. He wanted it for Dr. Merriam, on the chance that it might be a new species. While we all went fishing in the afternoon, the President skinned his mouse, and prepared the pelt to be sent to Washington. It was done as neatly as a professed taxidermist would have done it. This was the only game the President killed in the Park. In relating the incident to a reporter while I was in Spokane, the thought occurred to me, Suppose he changes that *u* to an *o*, and makes the President capture a moose, what a pickle I shall be in! Is it anything more than ordinary newspaper enterprise to turn a mouse into a moose? But, luckily for me, no such metamorphosis happened to that little mouse. It turned out not to be a new species, as it should have been, but a species new to the Park.

I caught trout that afternoon, on the edge of steaming pools in the Madison River that seemed to my hand almost blood-warm. I suppose they found better feeding where the water was warm. On the table they did not compare with our Eastern brook trout.

I was pleased to be told at one of the hotels that they had kalsomined some of the rooms with material from one of the devil's paint-pots. It imparted a soft, delicate, pinkish tint, not at all suggestive of things satanic.

One afternoon at Norris's, the President and I took a walk to observe the birds. In the grove about the barns there was a great number, the most attractive to me being the mountain bluebird. These birds we saw in all parts of the Park, and at Norris's there was an unusual number of them. How blue they were, — breast and all! In voice and manner they were almost identical with our bluebird. The Western purple finch was abundant here also, and juncos, and several kinds of sparrows, with an occasional Western robin. A pair of wild geese were feeding in the low, marshy ground not over one hundred yards from us, but when we tried to approach nearer they took wing. A few geese and ducks seem to winter in the Park.

The second morning at Norris's one of our teamsters, George Marvin, suddenly dropped dead from some heart affection, just as he had finished caring for his team. It was a great shock to us all. I never saw a better man with a team than he was. I had ridden on the seat beside him all the day previous. On one of the "formations" our teams had got mired in the soft, putty-like mud, and at one time it looked as if they could never extricate themselves, and I doubt if they could have, had it not been for the skill with which Marvin managed them. We started for the Grand Cañon up the Yellowstone that morning, and, in order to give myself a walk over the crisp snow in the clear, frosty air, I set out a little while in advance of the teams. As I did so, I saw the President, accompanied by one of the teamsters, walking hurriedly toward the barn to pay his last respects to the body of Marvin. After we had re-turned to Mammoth Hot Springs, he made inquiries for the young woman to whom he had been told that Marvin was engaged to be married. He looked her up, and sat a long time with her in her home, offering his sympathy, and speaking words of consolation. The act shows the depth and breadth of his humanity.

At the Cañon Hotel the snow was very deep, and had become so soft from the warmth of the earth beneath, as well as from the sun above, that we could only reach the brink of the Cañon on skis. The President and Major Pitcher had used skis before, but I had not, and, starting out without the customary pole, I soon came to grief. The snow gave way beneath me, and I was soon in an awk-ward predicament. The more I struggled, the lower my head and shoulders went, till only my heels, strapped to those long timbers, protruded above the snow. To reverse my position was impossible till some one came and reached me the end of a pole, and pulled me upright. But I very soon got the hang of the things, and the President and I quickly left the superintendent behind. I think I could have passed the President, but my manners forbade. He was heavier than I was, and broke in more. When one of his feet would go down half a yard or more, I noted with admiration the skilled diplomacy he displayed in extricating it. The tendency of my skis was all the time to diverge, and each to go off at an acute angle to my main course, and I had constantly to be on the alert to check this tendency.

Paths had been shoveled for us along the brink of the Cañon, so that we got the usual views from the different points. The Cañon was nearly free from snow, and was a grand spectacle, by far the grandest to be seen in the Park. The President told us that once, when pressed for meat, while returning through here from one of his hunting trips, he had made his way down to the river that we saw rushing along beneath us, and had caught some trout for dinner. Necessity alone could induce him to fish.

Across the head of the Falls there was a bridge of snow and ice, upon which we were told that the coyotes passed. As the season progressed, there would come a day when the bridge would not be safe. It would be interesting to know if the coyotes knew when this time arrived.

The only live thing we saw in the Cañon was an osprey perched upon a rock opposite us.

Near the falls of the Yellowstone, as at other places we had visited, a squad of soldiers had their winter quarters. The

President called on them, as he had called upon the others, looked over the books they had to read, examined their house-keeping arrangements, and conversed freely with them.

In front of the hotel were some low hills separated by gentle valleys. At the President's suggestion, he and I raced on our skis down those inclines. We had only to stand up straight, and let gravity do the rest. As we were going swiftly down the side of one of the hills, I saw out of the corner of my eye the President taking a header into the snow. The snow had given way beneath him, and nothing could save him from taking the plunge. I don't know whether I called out, or only thought, something about the down-fall of the administration. At any rate, the administration was down, and pretty well buried, but it was quickly on its feet again, shaking off the snow with a boy's

73

laughter. I kept straight on, and very soon the laugh was on me, for the treacherous snow sank beneath me, and I took a header, too.

"Who is laughing now, Oom John?" called out the President.

The spirit of the boy was in the air that day about the Cañon of the Yellowstone, and the biggest boy of us all was President Roosevelt.

The snow was getting so soft in the middle of the day that our return to the Mammoth Hot Springs could no longer be delayed. Accordingly, we were up in the morning, and ready to start on the home journey, a distance of twenty miles, by four o'clock. The snow bore up the horses well till mid-forenoon, when it began to give way beneath them. But by very careful management we pulled through without serious delay, and were back again at the house of Major Pitcher

74

in time for luncheon, being the only out-siders who had ever made the tour of the Park so early in the season.

A few days later I bade good-by to the President, who went on his way to Cali-fornia, while I made a loop of travel to Spokane, and around through Idaho and Montana, and had glimpses of the great, optimistic, sunshiny West that I shall not soon forget.

PRESIDENT ROOSEVELT AS A
NATURE–LOVER AND
OBSERVER

PRESIDENT ROOSEVELT
AS A NATURE–LOVER
AND OBSERVER

OUR many-sided President has a side
to his nature of which the public has
heard but little, and which, in view of
his recent criticism of what he calls the
nature fakirs, is of especial interest and
importance. I refer to his keenness and
enthusiasm as a student of animal life,
and his extraordinary powers of observation. The charge recently made against
him that he is only a sportsman and has
only a sportsman's interest in nature is
very wide of the mark. Why, I cannot
now recall that I have ever met a man
with a keener and more comprehensive
interest in the wild life about us — an
interest that is at once scientific and

thoroughly human. And by human I do not mean anything akin to the sentimentalism that sicklies o'er so much of our more recent natural history writing, and that inspires the founding of hospitals for sick cats; but I mean his robust, manly love for all open-air life, and his sympathetic insight into it. When I first read his "Wilderness Hunter," many years ago, I was impressed by his rare combination of the sportsman and the naturalist. When I accompanied him on his trip to the Yellowstone Park in April, 1903, I got a fresh impression of the extent of his natural history knowledge and of his trained powers of observation. Nothing escaped him, from bears to mice, from wild geese to chickadees, from elk to red squirrels; he took it all in, and he took it in as only an alert, vigorous mind can take it in. On that occasion I was able to help him identify only one new bird, as I have related in the foregoing chapter. All the other birds he recognized as quickly as I did.

During a recent half-day spent with the President at Sagamore Hill I got a still more vivid impression of his keenness and quickness in all natural history matters. The one passion of his life seemed natural history, and the appearance of a new warbler in his woods — new in the breeding season on Long Island — seemed an event that threw the affairs of state and of the presidential succession quite into the background. Indeed, he fairly bubbled over with delight at the thought of his new birds and at the prospect of showing them to his visitors. He said to my friend who accompanied me, John Lewis Childs, of Floral Park, a former State Senator, that he could not talk politics then, he wanted to talk and to hunt birds. And it was not long before he was as hot on the trail of that new warbler as he had recently been on the trail of some of the great trusts. Fancy a President of the United States stalking rapidly across bushy fields to the woods, eager as a boy and filled with the one idea of showing to his visitors the black-throated green warbler! We were presently in the edge of the woods and standing under a locust tree, where the President had several times seen and heard his rare visitant. "That's his note now," he said, and we all three recognized it at the same instant. It came from across a little valley fifty yards farther in the woods. We were soon standing under the tree in which the bird was singing, and presently had our glasses upon him.

"There is no mistake about it, Mr. President," we both said; "it is surely the black-throated green," and he laughed in glee. "I knew it could be no other;

82

THE PRESIDENT'S HOME ON SAGAMORE HILL, SHOWING ADDITION KNOWN AS
THE TROPHY ROOM

A BIT OF WOODLAND ON THE SLOPE TOWARDS OYSTER BAY

there is no mistaking that song and those markings. 'Trees, trees, murmuring trees!' some one reports him as saying. Now if we could only find the nest;" but we did not, though it was doubtless not far off.

Our warblers, both in color and in song, are bewildering even to the experienced ornithologist, but the President had mastered most of them. Not long before he had written me from Washington that he had just come in from walking with Mrs. Roosevelt about the White House grounds looking up arriving warblers. "Most of the warblers were up in the tops of the trees, and I could not get a good glimpse of them; but there was one with chestnut cheeks, with bright yellow behind the cheeks, and a yellow breast thickly streaked with black, which has puzzled me. Doubtless it is a very common kind which has for the moment slipped my memory. I saw the Blackburnian, the summer yellowbird, and the black-throated green." The next day he wrote me that he had identified the puzzling warbler; it was the Cape May. There is a tradition among newspaper men in Washington that a Cape May warbler once broke up a Cabinet meeting; maybe this was that identical bird.

At luncheon he told us of some of his ornithological excursions in the White House grounds, how people would stare at him as he stood gazing up into the trees like one demented. "No doubt they thought me insane." "Yes," said Mrs. Roosevelt, "and as I was always with him, they no doubt thought I was the nurse that had him in charge."

In his "Pastimes of an American Hunter" he tells of the owls that in June sometimes came after nightfall about the White House. "Sometimes they flew

84

noiselessly to and fro, and seemingly caught big insects on the wing. At other times they would perch on the iron awning bars directly overhead. Once one of them perched over one of the windows and sat motionless, looking exactly like an owl of Pallas Athene."

He knew the vireos also, and had seen and heard the white-eyed at his Virginia place, "Pine Knot," and he described its peculiar, emphatic song. As I moved along with the thought of this bird in mind and its snappy, incisive song, as I used to hear it in the old days near Washington, I fancied I caught its note in a dense bushy place below us. We paused to listen. "A catbird," said the President, and so we all agreed. We saw and heard a chewink. "Out West the chewink calls like a catbird," he observed. Continuing our walk, we skirted the edge of an orchard. Here the President called our

85

attention to a high-hole's nest in a cavity of an old apple tree. He rapped on the trunk of the tree that we might hear the smothered cry for food of the young inside. A few days before he had found one of the half-fledged young on the ground under the tree, and had managed to reach up and drop it back into the nest. "What a boiling there was in there," he said, "when the youngster dropped in!"

A cuckoo called in a tree overhead, the first I had heard this season. I feared the cold spring had cut them off. "The yellow-billed, undoubtedly," the President observed, and was confirmed by Mr. Childs. I was not certain that I knew the call of the yellow-billed from that of the black-billed. "We have them both," said the President, "but the yellow-billed is the more common."

We continued our walk along a path

that led down through a most delightful wood to the bay. Everywhere the marks of the President's axe were visible, as he had with his own hand thinned out and cleared up a large section of the wood.

A few days previous he had seen some birds in a group of tulip-trees near the edge of the woods facing the water; he thought they were rose-breasted grosbeaks, but could not quite make them out. He had hoped to find them there now, and we looked and listened for some moments, but no birds appeared.

Then he led us to a little pond in the midst of the forest where the night heron sometimes nested. A pair of them had nested there in a big water maple the year before, but the crows had broken them up. As we reached the spot the cry of the heron was heard over the tree-tops. "That is its alarm note," said the President. I remarked that it was much like

87

the cry of the little green heron. "Yes, it is, but if we wait here till the heron returns, and we are not discovered, you would hear his other more characteristic call, a hoarse quawk."

Presently we moved on along another path through the woods toward the house. A large, wide-spreading oak attracted my attention — a superb tree.

"You see by the branching of that oak," said the President, "that when it grew up this wood was an open field and maybe under the plough; it is only in fields that oaks take that form." I knew it was true, but my mind did not take in the fact when I first saw the tree. His mind acts with wonderful swiftness and completeness, as I had abundant proof that day.

As we walked along we discussed many questions, all bearing directly or indirectly upon natural history. The conversation was perpetually interrupted by some bird-

note in the trees about us which we would
pause to identify — the President's ear,
I thought, being the most alert of the
three. Continuing the talk, he dwelt upon
the inaccuracy of most persons' seeing,
and upon the unreliability as natural
history of most of the stories told by
guides and hunters. Sometimes writers
of repute were to be read with caution.
He mentioned that excellent hunting
book of Colonel Dodge's, in which are
described two species of the puma, one
in the West called the " mountain lion,"
very fierce and dangerous; the other called
in the East the "panther," —a harmless
and cowardly animal. "Both the same
species," said the President, " and almost
identical in disposition."

Nothing is harder than to convince a
person that he has seen wrongly. The
other day a doctor accosted me in the
street of one of our inland towns to tell

me of a strange bird he had seen; the bird was blood-red all over and was in some low bushes by the roadside. Of course I thought of our scarlet tanager, which was then just arriving. No, he knew that bird with black wings and tail; this bird had no black upon it, but every quill and feather was vivid scarlet. The doctor was very positive, so I had to tell him we had no such bird in our state. There was the summer redbird common in the Southern States, but this place is much beyond its northern limit, and, besides, this bird is not scarlet, but is of a dull red. Of course he had seen a tanager, but in the shade of the bushes the black of the wings and tail had escaped him.

This was simply a case of mis-seeing in an educated man; but in the untrained minds of trappers and woodsmen generally there is an element of the superstitious, and a love for the marvelous, which often prevents them from seeing the wild life about them just as it is. They possess the mythopœic faculty, and they unconsciously give play to it.

Thus our talk wandered as we wandered along the woods and field paths. The President brought us back by the corner of a clover meadow where he was sure a pair of red-shouldered starlings had a nest. He knew it was an unlikely place for starlings to nest, as they breed in marshes and along streams and in the low bushes on lake borders, but this pair had always shown great uneasiness when he had approached this plot of tall clover. As we drew near, the male starling appeared and uttered his alarm note. The President struck out to look for the nest, and for a time the Administration was indeed in clover, with the alarmed blackbird circling above it and showing great agitation. For my part, I hesitated on the edge of the clover patch, having a farmer's dread of seeing fine grass trampled down. I suggested to the President that he was injuring his hay crop; that the nest was undoubtedly there or near there; so he came out of the tall grass, and, after looking into the old tumbled-down barn — a regular early settler's barn, with huge timbers hewn from forest trees — that stood near by, and which the President said he preserved for its picturesqueness and its savor of old times, as well as for a place to romp in with his dogs and children, we made our way to the house.

The purple finch nested in the trees about the house, and the President was greatly pleased that he was able to show us this bird also.

A few days previous to our visit the children had found a bird's nest on the ground, in the grass, a few yards below

A PATH IN THE WOODS LEADING TO COLD SPRING HARBOR

A YEARLING IN THE APPLE ORCHARD

the front of the house. There were young birds in it, and as the President had seen the grasshopper sparrow about there, he concluded the nest belonged to it. We went down to investigate it, and found the young gone and two addled eggs in the nest. When the President saw those eggs, he said: "That is not the nest of the grasshopper sparrow, after all; those are the eggs of the song sparrow, though the nest is more like that of the vesper sparrow. The eggs of the grasshopper sparrow are much lighter in color — almost white, with brown specks." For my part, I had quite forgotten for the moment how the eggs of the little sparrow looked or differed in color from those of the song sparrow. But the President has so little to remember that he forgets none of these minor things! His bird-lore and wood-lore seem as fresh as if just learned.

93

I asked him if he ever heard that rare piece of bird music, the flight song of the oven-bird. "Yes," he replied, "we frequently hear it of an evening, while we are sitting on the porch, right down there at the corner of the woods." Now, this flight song of the oven-bird was unknown to the older ornithologists, and Thoreau, with all his years of patient and tireless watching of birds and plants, never identified it; but the President had caught it quickly and easily, sitting on his porch at Sagamore Hill. I believe I may take the credit of being the first to identify and describe this song — back in the old "Wake Robin" days.

In an inscription in a book the President had just given me he had referred to himself as my pupil. Now I was to be his pupil. In dealing with the birds I could keep pace with him pretty easily, and, maybe, occasionally lead him; but when we came to consider big game and the animal life of the globe, I was no-where. His experience with the big game has been very extensive, and his acquaint-ance with the literature of the subject is far beyond my own; and he forgets no-thing, while my memory is a sieve. In his study he set before me a small bronze elephant in action, made by the famous French sculptor Barye. He asked me if I saw anything wrong with it. I looked it over carefully, and was obliged to confess that, so far as I could see, it was all right. Then he placed before me another, by a Japanese artist. Instantly I saw what was wrong with the Frenchman's elephant. Its action was like that of a horse or a cow, or any trotting animal — a hind and a front foot on opposite sides mov-ing together. The Japanese had caught the real movement of the animal, which is that of a pacer — both legs on the same

95

side at a time. What different effects the two actions gave the statuettes! The free swing of the Japanese elephant you at once recognize as the real thing. The President laughed, and said he had never seen any criticism of Barye's elephant on this ground, or any allusion to his mistake; it was his own discovery. I was fairly beaten at my own game of observation.

He then took down a copy of his "Ranch Life and the Hunting Trail," and pointed out to me the mistakes the artist had made in some of his drawings of big Western game.

"Do you see anything wrong in the head of the pronghorn?" he asked, referring to the animal which the hunter is bringing in on the saddle behind him. Again I had to confess that I could not. Then he showed me the mounted head of a pronghorn over the mantel in one of his rooms, and called my attention to the

96

fact that the eye was close under the root of the horn, whereas in the picture the artist had placed it about two inches too low. And in the artist's picture of the pronghorn, which heads Chapter IX, he had made the tail much too long, as he had the tail of the elk on the opposite page.

I had heard of Mr. Roosevelt's attending a fair in Orange County, while he was Governor, where a group of mounted deer were exhibited. It seems the group had had rough usage, and one of the deer had lost its tail and a new one had been supplied. No one had noticed anything wrong with it till Mr. Roosevelt came along. "But the minute he clapped his eyes on that group," says the exhibitor, "he called out, 'Here, Gunther, what do you mean by putting a white-tail deer's tail on a black-tail deer?'" Such closeness and accuracy of observation even few naturalists can lay claim to. I mentioned the incident to him, and he recalled it laughingly. He then took down a volume on the deer family which he had himself had a share in writing, and pointed out two mistakes in the naming of the pictures which had been overlooked. The picture of the "white-tail in flight" was the black-tail of Colorado, and the picture of the black-tail of Colorado showed the black-tail of Columbia — the difference this time being seen in the branching of the horns.

The President took us through his house and showed us his trophies of the chase — bearskins of all sorts and sizes on the floors, panther and lynx skins on the chairs, and elk heads and deer heads on the walls, and one very large skin of the gray timber wolf. We examined the teeth of the wolf, barely more than an inch long, and we all laughed at the idea of its reaching the heart of a caribou through the breast by a snap, or any number of snaps, as it has been reported to do. I doubt if it could have reached the heart of a gobbler turkey in that way at a single snap.

The President's interest in birds, and in natural history generally, dates from his youth. While yet in his teens he published a list of the birds of Franklin County, New York. He showed me a bird journal which he kept in Egypt when he was a lad of fourteen, and a case of three African plovers which he had set up at that time; and they were well done.

Evidently one of his chief sources of pleasure at Sagamore Hill is the companionship of the birds. He missed the bobolink, the seaside finch, and the marsh wren, but his woods and grounds abounded in other species. He knew and

99

enjoyed not only all the more common birds, but many rarer and shyer ones that few country people ever take note of—such as the Maryland yellow-throat, the black and white creeper, the yellow-breasted chat, the oven-bird, the prairie warbler, the great crested flycatcher, the wood pewee, and the sharp-tailed finch. He enjoyed the little owls, too. "It is a pity the little-eared owl is called a screech owl. Its tremulous, quavering cry is not a screech at all, and has an attraction of its own. These little owls come up to the house after dark, and are fond of sitting on the elk's antlers over the gable. When the moon is up, by choosing one's position, the little owl appears in sharp outline against the bright disk, seated on his many-tined perch."

A few days after my visit he wrote me that he had identified the yellow-throated or Dominican warbler in his woods, the first he had ever seen. I had to confess to him that I had never seen the bird. It is very rare north of Maryland. The same letter records several interesting little incidents in the wild life about him:

"The other night I took out the boys in rowboats for a camping-out expedition. We camped on the beach under a low bluff near the grove where a few years ago on a similar expedition we saw a red fox. This time two young foxes, evidently this year's cubs, came around the camp half a dozen times during the night, coming up within ten yards of the fire to pick up scraps and seeming to be very little bothered by our presence. Yesterday on the tennis ground I found a mole shrew. He was near the side lines first. I picked him up in my handkerchief, for he bit my hand, and after we had all looked at him I let him go; but in a few minutes he came back and deliberately crossed the tennis grounds by the net. As he ran over the level floor of the court, his motion reminded all of us of the motion of those mechanical mice that run around on wheels when wound up. A chipmunk that lives near the tennis court continually crosses it when the game is in progress. He has done it two or three times this year, and either he or his predecessor has had the same habit for several years. I am really puzzled to know why he should go across this perfectly bare surface, with the players jumping about on it, when he is not frightened and has no reason that I can see for going. Apparently he grows accustomed to the players and moves about among them as he would move about, for instance, among a herd of cattle."

The President is a born nature-lover, and he has what does not always go with this passion — remarkable powers of observation. He sees quickly and surely, not less so with the corporeal eye than with the mental. His exceptional vitality, his awareness all around, gives the clue to his powers of seeing. The chief qualification of a born observer is an alert, sensitive, objective type of mind, and this Roosevelt has in a preëminent degree.

You may know the true observer, not by the big things he sees, but by the little things; and then not by the things he sees with effort and premeditation, but by his effortless, unpremeditated seeing— the quick, spontaneous action of his mind in the presence of natural objects. Everybody sees the big things, and anybody can go out with note-book and opera-glass and make a dead set at the birds, or can go into the northern forests and interview guides and trappers and Indians, and stare in at the door of the " school of the woods." None of these things evince powers of observation; they only evince industry and intention. In fact, born observers are about as rare as born poets. Plenty of men can see straight and report straight what they see; but the men who see what others miss, who see quickly and surely, who have the detective eye, like Sherlock Holmes, who "get the drop," so to speak, on every object, who see minutely and who see whole, are rare indeed.

President Roosevelt comes as near fulfilling this ideal as any man I have known. His mind moves with wonderful celerity, and yet as an observer he is very cautious, jumps to no hasty conclusions.

He had written me, toward the end of May, that while at Pine Knot in Virginia he had seen a small flock of passenger pigeons. As I had been following

up the reports of wild pigeons from vari-
ous parts of our own state during the
past two or three years, this statement of
the President's made me prick up my
ears. In my reply I said, "I hope you are
sure about those pigeons," and I told
him of my interest in the subject, and
also how all reports of pigeons in the
East had been discredited by a man in
Michigan who was writing a book on the
subject. This made him prick up his
ears, and he replied that while he felt very
certain he had seen a small band of the
old wild pigeons, yet he might have been
deceived; the eye sometimes plays one
tricks. He said that in his old ranch days
he and a cowboy companion thought one
day that they had discovered a colony of
black prairie dogs, thanks entirely to the
peculiar angle at which the light struck
them. He said that while he was President he did not want to make any state-

ment, even about pigeons, for the truth of which he did not have good evidence. He would have the matter looked into by a friend at Pine Knot upon whom he could depend. He did so, and convinced himself and me also that he had really seen wild pigeons. I had the pleasure of telling him that in the same mail with his letter came the news to me of a large flock of wild pigeons having been seen near the Beaverkill in Sullivan County, New York. While he was verifying his observation I was in Sullivan County verifying this report. I saw and questioned persons who had seen the pigeons, and I came away fully convinced that a flock of probably a thousand birds had been seen there late in the afternoon of May 23. "You need have no doubt about it," said the most competent witness, an old farmer. "I lived here when the pigeons nested here in count-

HALLWAY, SAGAMORE HILL.

less numbers forty years ago. I know pigeons as I know folks, and these were pigeons."

I mention this incident of the pigeons because I know that the fact that they have been lately seen in considerable numbers will be good news to a large number of readers.

The President's nature-love is deep and abiding. Not every bird student succeeds in making the birds a part of his life. Not till you have long and sympathetic intercourse with them, in fact, not till you have loved them for their own sake, do they enter into and become a part of your life. I could quote many passages from President Roosevelt's books which show how he has felt and loved the birds, and how discriminating his ear is with regard to their songs. Here is one:—

"The meadow-lark is a singer of a

higher order [than the plains skylark], deserving to rank with the best. Its song has length, variety, power, and rich melody, and there is in it sometimes a cadence of wild sadness inexpressibly touching. Yet I cannot say that either song would appeal to others as it appeals to me; for to me it comes forever laden with a hundred memories and associations — with the sight of dim hills reddening in the dawn, with the breath of cool morning winds blowing across lonely plains, with the scent of flowers on the sunlit prairie, with the motion of fiery horses, with all the strong thrill of eager and buoyant life. I doubt if any man can judge dispassionately the bird-songs of his own country; he cannot disassociate them from the sights and sounds of the land that is so dear to him."

Here is another, touching upon some European song-birds as compared with

some of our own: "No one can help liking the lark; it is such a brave, honest,
cheery bird, and moreover its song is uttered in the air, and is very long-sustained.
But it is by no means a musician of the
first rank. The nightingale is a performer
of a very different and far higher order; yet though it is indeed a notable and
admirable singer, it is an exaggeration
to call it unequaled. In melody, and
above all in that finer, higher melody
where the chords vibrate with the touch
of eternal sorrow, it cannot rank with
such singers as the wood-thrush and
the hermit-thrush. The serene ethereal
beauty of the hermit's song, rising and
falling through the still evening, under
the archways of hoary mountain forests
that have endured from time everlasting;
the golden, leisurely chiming of the wood-
thrush, sounding on June afternoons,
stanza by stanza, through the sun-flecked

groves of tall hickories, oaks, and chest-
nuts; with these there is nothing in the
nightingale's song to compare. But in
volume and continuity, in tuneful, volu-
ble, rapid outpouring and ardor, above
all in skillful and intricate variation of
theme, its song far surpasses that of
either of the thrushes. In all these respects it is more just to compare it with
the mocking-bird's, which, as a rule, likewise falls short precisely on those points
where the songs of the two thrushes
excel."

In his "Pastimes of an American
Hunter" he says: "It is an incalculable
added pleasure to any one's sense of hap-
piness if he or she grows to know, even
slightly and imperfectly, how to read and
enjoy the wonder-book of nature. All
hunters should be nature-lovers. It is to
be hoped that the days of mere wasteful,
boastful slaughter are past, and that

from now on the hunter will stand fore-
most in working for the preservation and
perpetuation of the wild life, whether big
or little." Surely this man is the rarest
kind of a sportsman.